THE DISTANCE LEARNING WORKBOOK

Hands On Approach To Virtual Teaching

KHAREN MINASIAN
DEBRA KIDDER

CONTENTS

HANDS ON APPROACH TO VIRTUAL TEACHING (PT 3)

I would like to first say "Thank You" to our wonderful partner and educator Debra Kidder. Her passion for teaching, wisdom, and ability to deliver information in an organized and easily implementable way is truly a gift.

It is my honor to have Debra on the STORM team because she resembles exactly what our organization is built upon. Special Team Of Role Models is on a mission to provide parents and educators with the best and most current resources available.

We hope that you enjoy this book and will implement many of the tactics presented in an effort to make your distance learning journey a great success.

At the end of the book, you will find links and information to other STORM resources that we believe you will find very useful.

Thank you

Kharen Minasian
Co-Founder
www.stormprogram.com

QUICK START GUIDE TO DISTANCE LEARNING

Top Five Hallmarks of Distance Teaching:
- Distance teaching is student centered
- Distance teaching means relationships with students are prioritized over introduction of content
- Distance teaching requires real world connections to curriculum to make learning meaningful to students
- Distance teaching makes use of cooperative student learning after teacher led presentation of big ideas and essential questions
- Distance teaching relies of student demonstration of mastery in may forms, and not solely exams and papers for assessments

Top Five Early Distance Learning Points to Remember:
- Relationships over content
- Connections over testing
- Your digital classroom space is a village
- Encourage student agency everyday
- Keep teacher led time limited, and student centered learning should be the centerpiece of the school day

. . .

Top Five Distance Learning Classroom Space Tips:
- Your online classroom should look neat and be consistent from day to day.
- Post your contact information (with your preferred method noted) clearly.
- Links to information and assignments should be easy to find and open with a single click.
- Use breakout rooms and software that promotes cooperative learning to support student centered learning
- Remember that seat time in the digital environment *does not* transfer 1:1 to the online environment

Top Five Morning Student Engagement Techniques:
- Log into your classroom early and have soft music playing to create a gentle entry for your students.
- Start (and end) your day with a slogan, a saying, or a cheer that the students have created or agreed upon.
- Spend an early part of your day on social emotional learning activities.
- Use a quote of the day, or a song lyric, posted in the students' field of vision to anchor your teaching for the day. At some point during the day, pivot to the quote and ask your students what they think it means, or to re-state it.
- Use each students' name at least once before lunch.

Top Five Re-Engagement Activities (Excellent for Use After Specials, Lunch, or Whenever the Class Seems Antsy or Needs to Re-Focus):
- Scavenger Hunt for odd items around the house (5 items or less to limit time)
- Group artwork--based on a photo projected by you, or a free draw, or any art created while you read literature or poetry
- Journaling, using the writing prompts in Part 2, Unit 10
- Show a short video on a current event, a TedTalk, or something simply funny and enjoyable--that can promote a discussion and focus

• Breathing and stretching exercises, found on YouTube or TeacherTube

Top Five Ways to Reign in a Class When You Feel You Are Losing Them:
• Call on students by name.
• Change topics/subjects quickly to grab their attention.
• Shift gears and engage in a cooperative learning activity using online software.
• Take a deep breath, and remember that the students have silly days, also. Put on music to change the atmosphere.
• Go completely off book and try something new and untested. Call on a student to continue the class if the students are older, use "show me thumbs up if you can hear what I am saying.....put your finger on your nose if you an hear what I am saying....both hands on your head if you can hear what I am saying...." if students are younger.

Top Five Ways to End The Day On A Bright Note:
• Give a quick, upbeat recap of the best events of the day
• Give a shout out to students who met a goal or high achievement for the day.
• Tell students at least one positive event, topic, or project to look forward to the following day.
• Smile when you sign off for the day.
• Use a short song, cheer, slogan or saying that the class has created or decided upon together.

Top Five Ways to Shift Your Planning to be Efficient and Student Centered:
• Your role as teacher is the Guide on the Side; keep teacher led time to a minimum
• Present big ideas and essential questions, then move to student

activity, consisting of group work, breakout rooms, digital presentation creations, and/or student led Q&A sessions

• Seat time does not transfer 1:1 from in person to online learning, plan accordingly

• Remove any 'fluff,' 'time filling,'or 'extra' activities

• Be available to ask guiding questions and answer student requests for more information, but allow students to search for and discover information

Top Five Digital Presentation/Project Creators:
• PrexiNext
• Venngage
• Google Slides
• PowerPoint
• Visme

Top Five Feedback Questions:
• Can you easily find what you need in the classroom?
• Are my assignments and due dates clear?
• Are you comfortable asking questions?
• Do you feel that you are being heard?
• How would you improve this experience?

Top Five Ways to Generate Parental Involvement:
• Hold parental office hours
• Hold a cultural awareness event online and invite parents to share
• Reach out to parents via phone and/or email weekly with personal updates on their student
• Use the Remind app or a similar product to keep communication flowing. Involvement starts with easy communication
• Start a Parents Club, with a weekly or monthly check in meeting online to coordinate events and/or gather supplies for the students

. . .

Top Five Writing Prompts for Students:
- The greatest movie ever is...
- My favorite scent is...
- The most awesome relative I have is....
- An assignment I wish you would give is...
- If I could be anywhere right now it would be...

Top Five Social Emotional Learning Activities (from Part 3, Unit 2):
- Simply ask students to write three words that describe how they feel. Students want to be seen and heard. This simple activity accomplishes that.
- Pizza Man
- Wisdom Wednesdays
- Emotion Detective
- Reflection Fridays

Top Five Virtual Field Trips:
- NASA Mars Exploration
- Lourve Museum in Paris
- Hiking the Great Wall of China
- Royal Tour of Buckingham Palace
- Google Arts and Culture National Parks Tour

HANDS ON APPROACH TO VIRTUAL TEACHING (PT 1)

UNIT 1: YOUR DISTANCE TEACHING PRE PLAN

E verything is going to be OK.

Maybe you are reading this because you find yourself suddenly teaching online, with little or no formal training, and you're looking for real, hands on help.

Maybe you chose to start teaching remotely,, and you want some solid advice on how to do it to the best of your ability.

Maybe you are reading this because you are curious as to how all this distance teaching works, and works well.

You are in great company. Thousands of educators moved to online teaching in the spring of 2020 because of the global pandemic, but online teaching has existed since the start of the Internet, and distance learning has been around since the Pony Express.

This book will give you a little of the background you need to understand why distance teaching can work. But more importantly, this book gives you **practical guidance and hands-on activities so you know what to do to make distance teaching work and work well.**

You've heard the phrase "Work smarter, not harder?"

Stop spinning your wheels. Teaching online doesn't need to feel like an impossible task.

I know this because, believe it or not, I lived a microcosm of an educational world turned upside down in the blink of an eye, when no one could see anything but disaster, and it all turned it out fine.

About eight years ago, my son's school flooded. It was the middle of a particularly cold New England winter, and a ceiling pipe burst in his one level elementary school in the first few days of winter recess. The alarm that should have alerted the building staff never sounded. The cold water seeped into every classroom, pulling up tiles as it went, bringing down the ceiling entirely over five classrooms.

When the staff and students returned in early January, there was panic and confusion. Students were sent home. Clean up began--only to uncover the broken tiles contained asbestos, and that abatement would take the remainder of the year.

The administration scrambled to find a way to continue the education of the students with as little disruption as possible; the temporary fix was to divide the students in grades 1-6 between the remaining elementary schools, whose class sizes jumped from around 20 to 35 for three weeks.

While our students sat in cramped classrooms, sometimes on the floor, many times not having the materials they needed, the administrators looked for a more permanent solution; in stepped Yale University. You can look this part up, it is all a matter of public record.

Yale University, thankfully, had a building meant for office spaces they had not yet moved into. It was slightly removed from their downtown New Haven campus, close to our Orange suburb, straddling the West Haven line. Yale was graciously willing to share their space. The building was six stories tall and connected to their School of Nursing. They generously offered it for our use--but it in no way resembled an elementary school.

Being an office space, the floor plans were open. I mean, *really* open. Whole grades were assigned to big open spaces, and teachers were left to arrange whatever furniture wasn't destroyed in the flood to try to carve out an area for their group. (Side Bar--the 'Open Floor Plan' learning experiment had been attempted in western US in the 1990s and a few districts were still holding onto this teaching style, but it had faded from popularity by 2014.)

Teachers could hear each other giving instruction all day. They tried to put posters on the walls, work without computers, basic supplies, a cafeteria, a library, a playground, and any materials they previously had at the fingertips to support their curriculum. Copiers? Chromebooks? Even personal belongings? The flood had ruined just about everything.

What they had were the happy faces of their students looking to them for guidance, their knowledge of teaching, and a desire to make it work without going insane in the process.

The teachers of Peck Place School in Orange, Connecticut in 2014 were incredibly successful in the (admittedly smaller and less scary) face of their new teaching paradigm, thrust onto them whether they liked it or not; and you will, too.

Sound familiar?

Here we go.

UNIT 2: PREPARING FOR YOUR FIRST DAY OF DISTANCE TEACHING

In the spring of 2020, when the pandemic hit, teachers had to move into what I like to call emergency remote teaching. Do what you can from a distance, keep the kids learning, and you have X number of days and X number of meetings to figure this out.....right off the top, I can tell you this: good teaching is good teaching, in all its forms and deliveries. Be confident that you had it together going into this, and of course you can keep it together to keep going.

Distance learning is *not nearly the same thing* as in person learning. So it follows that distance teaching is *not nearly the same thing* as in person teaching. Seat time, assessments, interactions, it all needs to change. But it can be done just as well. This workbook will show you how to be a fantastic remote teacher with plans, activities, and ideas.

In all likelihood, distance teaching is a trend that is here to stay. Home schooling and distance teaching will become a standard part of American public school education. Distance teaching has existed for centuries for various reasons, and I truly believe that distance teaching will only grow in popularity. Very few colleges, universities, or higher institutions of learning currently offer degrees in distance learning; states do not yet offer licenses for it. That is coming. In the meantime,

we are here, in the trenches with you, to bring you up to speed on the important tenets of distance learning, how to deliver it to your students, and how to thrive while perfecting it.

UNIT 3: YOUR TEACHING SPACE, THEIR LEARNING SPACE

L et's start at the very, very beginning. Your school or district has announced that you are engaging in distance teaching either entirely or as part of a blended schedule. First, you need **a place to BE, to TEACH,** and that space is important. If you are teaching from your own home, find an area, *well lit,* where you have all of your supplies within easy reach. You probably want to turn a desk to face a window for natural (flattering, let's say it) lighting and nothing distracting behind you. A close, vertical space behind you is recommended for posting your daily goals, expectations, and for younger students, perhaps a planned stretch or snack break. While my son, a high schooler, is home remote learning, we were able to find an inexpensive, magnetized white board because he is a visual learner, and he is able to sketch out his schedule, his work, list his homework and other important due dates at his fingertips; this is a great idea for teachers working from home as well. Putting this information behind you to broadcast (visually) on a whiteboard every time you are on the screen will subliminally stick with your students. When they wonder about their homework, they will instinctively know where to look.

Other set up advice: raise your computer monitor so you avoid looking *down* while teaching, students will quickly capitalize on those moments. If possible, use a wireless keyboard and mouse to keep your workspace as neat as possible. Neat desk, neat mind. Remember to look into your camera, *not* your own image. When you look at yourself, you are not making eye contact with your students. Eye contact contributes to the feeling that you are with your mentally students when you are physically apart. This might take some practice. Try taking a selfie, and consciously look at yourself. Then take another while looking straight into the camera. Do you see the huge difference that makes to the viewer? In the first selfie, you will seem distracted. In the second, you are focused on the students.

Also, teachers are professionals. Dress the part. How you appear to your students and their families, no matter which grade you teach, will project how you feel about your position. However you would normally appear while teaching in person is how you should appear on screen. Your students are in the same pandemic as you; they are looking to the adults in their life for calm and normalcy, and that includes their teachers. Seeing you playing your part in their lives can be incredibly soothing, resulting in better engagement and therefore, achievement. If students are not distracted by the, let's face it, uncertainty even the youngest students among us are exposed to, the better chance you have of keeping their attention, and keeping it longer. Limiting distractions is good advice for any teaching scenario.

Lighting is also important, so investing in a light that attaches to your phone as it sits on your camera to brighten your face without blinding (checkout lumecube.com and others like it) is worth every penny. Not only will you look better, but you will subliminally become the star of the show in your students' minds, and that spotlight feeling will give you courage to be on camera. Pro tip: make sure you practice with it first. Make videos of yourself teaching, and test for audio and video clarity.

While you cannot control your students' homes, or create the ideal workspace for them, take the time at the start of the year to **encourage them to find a space** with a work surface that will mentally prepare them to learn. Ask them where they feel comfortable learning (the worst wrong answer--in front of the TV.) The younger the students are, the less likely they will inherently know that keeping pencils close by will save time later. This seems obvious to you, but this kind of thinking is not obvious to a six year old. Make your expectations for the day clear, and invite students into a conversation around a productive learning space. It can and likely will look very different from home to home. Let students know what they will need nearby, perhaps when they have stretch breaks (or a 'bell schedule') visible for older students.

- Your teaching space needs to be well lit, facing natural lighting, neat, and free from distractions
- Have a vertical space, preferably a magnetized white board near/behind you to create and post visuals for your students
- Have all your supplies within reach
- Neat space, neat mind
- Take the time to teach your students how to set up their work space
- Make your student space expectations clear; at minimum, they will need a dedicated horizontal surface
- Have an age appropriate conversation about work space productivity and avoiding distractions

UNIT 4: THE ONLINE CLASSROOM/DIGITAL TEACHING SPACE

There is a lot to be said for setting up your digital classroom. There are so many Learning Management Systems out there now, in light of recent events, and most teachers do not have a choice of which they would choose. Google Classroom is very popular, because of its ease of use and suite of products that integrate so easily (Slides, the new and wonderful Jamboard, PearDeck, etc). Blackboard and Moodle are still popular. Even Canvas has its own LMS. I recently learned that some districts are creating their own spaces from scratch. Whatever your school or district is using to organize learning, get to know all the bells and whistles of it. Watch YouTube videos. Consult your mentor/administrator/colleague. Ask questions. This is the time for inquiry. No one expects you to be an expert in this or any aspect of remote teaching (except, as always, that small group of parents who think they could do it all better no matter what you do). Write down your questions. If a student asks you something you don't know about the system, how things will proceed in class, and you do not know the answer, do not fake it. Even very young kids can tell when their trusted adult is not being truthful--tell them what you are doing to figure it out, who you are asking, and how long you think it will take before you can give them a solid response. **Keep your learning space neat,**

inviting, but not overwhelming, and keep live links grouped in one consistent spot. Remember: every click should lead to an activity or assignment. ONE. CLICK. Every additional click is an opportunity for a student to get lost.

- Get to know your LMS--YouTube videos and mentors are helpful
- Write down questions as you go--no one is an expert on the first day
- Use as few clicks as possible for each assignment and activity
- Keep live links together, and keep the most important documents at the top/near the front of your teaching space
- Keep your contact information easy to see at all times

UNIT 5: CONTENT DOES NOT COME FIRST--BUT WHY?

A quick, quick word about content here, because it will be covered in depth later on: In quality remote teaching, content is not the priority in the beginning. I know, I know. It seems counter intuitive. I became a teacher, specifically a music teacher, because first, I have a deep love and appreciation for music, and second, because I wanted to share that with others. I never did want to be a performer as most kids who love their lessons and practice time do, but I adored the idea of spreading the love of music. However, in remote learning, connection is a higher priority than any content, especially at the start of a new school year. Many of the teachers and students are working in learning through remote means reluctantly; this makes connection all the more important. The small, incidental ways teachers connect with students everyday in person cannot happen at a distance.

When distance teaching begins, these connections have to be intentionally programmed into your lessons; they actually need to *be* your lessons to start. If you do not connect with the students and show them how what you are teaching them connects with their lives outside of teaching time, nothing you teach them will be retained. Your content IS important. But if you are teaching and no students are engaged and therefore not earning, are you really teaching? Students will not stay engaged by your sheer will. This leads to two very important segments.

- Content is important--just not *yet*
- Connection and relationship building MUST come before content
- Relationships are the priority at the start of distance teaching
- Relationships are the priority at the start of distance teaching
- Yes I said that twice on purpose--I am stressing the importance of building relationships in distance teaching

UNIT 6: CONSISTENCY IS KEY IN DISTANCE TEACHING

No matter the age or grade, even if this is not dictated by your school or district, always start and end at the same time each day. Greet your students, by name, at the start of every day. Know that each day is a reset, a re-start, and even though the students are the same people, their behavior is shaped by dozens of events that occurred between the last time you saw them and when they logged on. Their lives have been turned upside down, just like yours. In a world where nothing is the same for them, be a safe place where they can rely on some form of consistency. Starting the day the same way, with connection and not content, even as the year progresses, encourages community (with traditions and belonging), which reinforces connection in a remote learning classroom.

- Start and end the day with routine--ideas to follow
- Greet students by name--make connections
- Be the consistency in their lives

UNIT 7: ENGAGEMENT COMES FIRST IN DISTANCE TEACHING

In quality online teaching, student centered learning is prioritized over everything, and to make that happen, connections are valued over everything else. If you cannot connect with each student, AND connect what you are teaching to how important your content is or will be beyond the classroom, computer screen, or school day, engagement will be nearly impossible. On the flip side, if you can show them how your lesson/unit/goal of the day connects somehow to the pop icon they live and breathe, the profession they aspire to join one day, the culture whose origin is evident in their clothes and music, you've made a valuable connection that will keep the students 'tuning in' day after day. Your classroom will become their safe community. We will discuss many ways to accomplish this, but a few quick ideas come to mind that you can use even before day one: use polls, pop culture questions, personalized emails to show your interest in the student beyond their experience in your class. The extra time and energy put up front will pay off later.

Personally, I always check with the National Day Calendar, which lists the "National Day," such as "National Pizza Topping Day," and I would take a few minutes during attendance to ask each student their favorite pizza topping. My students (who ranged in age from 11-18 at the time) soon knew to expect this and sometimes would beat me to it, asking me about my favorite things first. In this way I felt my classroom was more of a community, a village, which is another important part of remote teaching that we will discuss later. (more on the 'how' of engagement, and using the National Calendar Day as an example, later as well.)

- Engagement is as important as consistency and connections in the remote classroom
- If your classroom has the positivity of a community, students will *want* to be there, decreasing the need for management on your end
- Knowing your students 'favorite things' is an important part of connection, incorporating their favorite things into whatever you teach makes students *want* to be a part of your classroom community

UNIT 8: YOUR FIRST DAY ONLINE--HOW TO START, WITH ICE BREAKERS YOU CAN USE EVERYDAY

Have community building, get-to-know-your-class games ready to play. Some ideas for fresh, new get to know you games that you can use right away are:

1. Caption the Picture: Whether you find an interesting picture on the Internet or you have a funny picture in your personal collection, post it on the screen and give the students ten to twenty seconds to write a funny and witty caption to go with it. Personally, I have a picture of my daughter when she was two, asleep in her car seat with her finger up her nose. The captions I read out loud from that picture alone had my classes rolling with laughter on day one, and nothing bonds a new group like laughing together. Silly baby and animal pictures seem to work best, along with exhilarating, winning sports moments, in my experience.

2. Meme Mondays: every Monday, ask students to find and post the most inspirational, serious or comical, uplifting messages to get everyone ready to start the week. Students and teachers alike tend to drag into school in the morning, so finding a string of motivational memes in the digital

classroom is both bonding and helpful for the students and the teacher.

3. Guess the Recipe: this was a radio contest that always cracked me up. Find a recipe for something pretty ordinary--pancakes, chocolate chip cookies, roast beef--and read the ingredient list. Have the students guess what those ingredients could possibly create. Make the recipes more complicated as the year goes on.....

4. Where Am I?: In Zoom, and on Google Meet, you can digitally change your background....but you don't see it. You can do this with free images provided to you or images you upload yourself. Randomly choose one and click on it without looking (this may take some practice) and allow students to describe to you where you are.....without actually telling you. You then have to guess where you are. A dessert? The North pole? The Empire State Building? Make it more interesting by telling students they can't use words that start with S....or they can *only* use words that start with S to describe where you are.

5. A Boring Fact: Sharing anything personal can make even the most bold student feel pressured. This new twist removes some of that pressure because the point is to be boring--yet not repetitive. So while one student's favorite color may be blue, tell your students to have two or three back up boring facts ready; there should be no repeats. And who couldn't think up three boring facts about themselves? I like the flavor vanilla. I hate bedtime. I wish it was still summer. There. Easy and low pressure. The fresh twist is that 1) students cannot say anything that has already been said and 2) students cannot say anything they have said before.

UNIT 9: WAYS TO KEEP REMOTE STUDENTS ENGAGED-- TECHNIQUES TO USE NOW

1. Engagement starts from the first moment. Having soft music playing during the five minute buffer while you are logged on and students join creates a calm entry into class and a change in mindset from 'home' to 'learning time.' The music also passively engages the students into your remote classroom before the activity begins, and when it stops, that is an auditory signal to the students that class activity is beginning.

2. Starting with a Good Morning Class or a repeated morning catchphrase, something the students know to listen for each day, is one way to get your students to look at you. If you feel you do not have all of the students' attention, calling students by name who are still not dialed in, kindly, ("Good morning, Mary, thanks for joining us!") is another good idea. Do *not* wait for silence.

3. Keep your teacher-led time fast paced. This would include the time you spend opening the day (or your class period), your lesson big ideas, and your closings. Have your materials ready to go, and reduce downtime as much as possible.

Remember, quality distance teaching is *student centered*, even as young as kindergarten.

4. As mentioned earlier, The National Day Calendar (https://nationaldaycalendar.com/read/) never let me down for engaging ideas, especially for starting the day or putting a fun spin on attendance taking. There are usually three or four official National Days. For example, April 28th is National Blueberry Pie Day. So no matter what age student I have, either during morning meetings or class openings, I could ask if the student likes blueberry pie (and if not, which kind do they like?). Then ask that student to ask the next student and so on ... while I am taking attendance and suddenly, attendance is done. Older students might want to mention the last time they ate pie, made pie, tried a crazy kind of pie, etc. An activity like this will have your students wondering each day how class will begin, who will call on them, and who will they call on? This tradition bonds the class and traditions feed a community feel. When your class is running at a distance, having a community feel increases engagement and a sense of belonging, increasing a student's chances for success.

5. Later in the year, when things are rolling along into content, you may want to use **K/W/L Charts**. Knowledge/Wish To Learn/Learned Today Charts (a sort of entrance ticket, an informal assessment) will inform you with what the students already know about a topic so you don't waste valuable time re-teaching; you also avoid the risk of dis-engagement due to boredom. K/W/L charts are far from new, but are still considered a useful way to gage your students' understanding of a topic and keep them engaged. Not knowing what they already know and re-teaching it *decreases engagement*. This tool allows you to assess where the students are and where to start teaching them 'new.' Anything old and boring will cue disengagement. Great conversations about your subject have arisen from K/W/L charts, and when you finally start teaching content (or dive into the new

unit), students already feel armed and prepared. Also, there's that feeling of community that's encouraged, and you want that wherever you can.

6. If a student has experience in your content area (or you are at the point where you are introducing a new unit), give that student time to share. Remember, student centered learning means you are the "Guide On The Side" as often as possible, and the students are learning from each other where they can. Students can ask each other questions, and you can ask guiding questions and steer the conversation back when you are ready. The benefits? Again, traditions, community, engagement. Students can collaborate on a Google doc or some other idea sharing platform, because collaboration also fosters community.

7. Other ideas to build engagement and community in your remote classroom: **book clubs and virtual field trips** that pertain to your content area. Student run clubs and events like field trips, even virtual, can only bolster engagement.

8. Social Emotional Learning Activities will work well in this space as well, especially with middle and older students. I worked in a high school for years where the first experience of the day was called CPR. This 20 minute block was dedicated time for students to have a 'soft landing' into the environment for learning. Twenty minutes may be too long a period of time to spend in your learning space, but even ten minutes in the morning to address SEL is important. Try opening your day (or class) with a SEL activity to bond your group and set a positive mood in your class.

A sk students to think of three words, which can be related or non related to answer this question: How are you today? On the board behind you, or even on a piece of paper you hold on the screen, you can have words in columns or color coded from which the students can choose: simpler emotions for younger students, more complex for older students. They then write the words that best express how they are. Simple. The point is, someone is asking them, they know someone wants to know. For many students, showing up for school is motivated by the need to be seen and heard; knowing this is one of the first things you may do will encourage students to engage in your daily activities. You are showing your students you see them and want to hear from them. That is the first step to really knowing them, an essential part of connecting in distance learning. Specific SEL activities appear in Part 2.

1. Students K-12 have benefitted from this activity in my classrooms--draw your morning. After attendance, I've asked students to grab a piece of paper (or use a digital media, addressed in volume 2). Who knows what happened in your students' lives between alarm and class time? Maybe nothing important, maybe something major....you asking the question and wanting an answer shows the students you care, and you want them to know about each other as well.

2. Class Jigsaw Puzzles have worked well for me at every level. You can easily insert a blank jigsaw puzzle piece onto a Google Doc and post it in your classroom. Students can download, possibly print out and fill in with the information they want to share--remember, we encourage student agency in an age appropriate fashion. Starting with name, possibly birthdate, favorite things/colors, etc., are popular ways to decorate the puzzle piece. Once the pieces are returned to you (digitally or through the actual mail), you can decide to cut and place together and post so the students can see it whenever you are on camera, and/or you can put it together on a Google Doc and post it digitally in your classroom and you students can see it, connected, daily. I've done a similar activity with Venn Diagrams (both lo-tech with paper and pen, and high tech with Venngage), and overlapped circles where students wrote similar items about themselves.

3. Quote of the Day activities interest students of all ages, because while you provide a quote (from thousands of online sites or any book of famous quotes lying around), the

students provide the perspective and translation. All of us see life through our own personal perspective, shaped by our experiences and beliefs; so when we are presented with a single statement, it may be interpreted many ways. An interesting SEL activity would be to introduce your class to a quote and ask each of them to share an interpretation and how that quote relates to their lives.

4. Where We Came From is a great sharing game, and if you can contact your students before class begins you can begin day 1. Collect baby pictures, either by email or hard copy, and each morning show one at several points during the day. By the end of the day, ask students to identify the baby in the picture--and remember to include a picture of yourself! We are creating a community here!

UNIT 10: MOVEMENT ACTIVITIES TO RE-ENGAGE YOUR REMOTE CLASS

You're going to need more than some quick engaging attendance activities at the start of the day. These activities are meant either for the beginning of the year community building, or content work breaks when you sense the students need to stand up, move, and re-focus again.

a. The Wave. If you're old like me (er.....older) you can clearly remember being at a professional sports event, in a stadium, and somehow, someone started The Wave. Everyone in one section would stand up, hands over head, and that motion was usually accompanied by a vocalization that sounded like everyone was on a roller coaster. This motion would move *horizontally* around the stadium several times, and whenever I was a part of it the community feeling it inspired never ceased to amaze me. Believe it or not, this feeling can translate several ways to students on a screen. To build community further, **don't** be the leader. Show your students a video of what the wave was, and ask how *they* think it could transfer to the current situation. This is a great community building, cooperative learning opportunity for them, with you as the Guide On The Side, perhaps offering a subtle nudge here and there.

b. Freeze Dance. Tried and true, always a hit with the littles, even older kids will get into Freeze Dance if **one of them is allowed to play DJ**. One of the benefits to having your students on a computer is that they have access to their music library. Let them share that part of themselves with the class. Kick it up a notch: when the music stops, add a task, like strike a model's pose! Or, salute like a soldier! Or, hands in the air! You get the picture.

c. Group Art. My kids, both bio and students, loved this activity while learning from a distance. Ask your students to grab some plain white paper and any colorful art supplies that want to work with--pencils, crayons, markers, or paint. Then, using your words only, you will read or describe to them an object or event and they will create what you are saying in art. In the end, they are invited to hold up their great works, and even better--display them in the background of their home school space as a badge of a group project to promote community. The best thing about this project is that it can be done more than once and the literature can change from silly to dark to informative, and the reader can change as well. This activity can be woven into the weekly routine of your class as a bonding activity.

d. Scavenger Hunt. When students are really antsy and need to get away from their screen and focus their eyes on a real object, this is the activity you want. The list of things to find needs to be age appropriate and fresh. An updated twist is that after every few items are located, determine which object might have a story attached and ask about it. Search hard for lists of seriously random things your students will enjoy locating. A living thing? That would include siblings or plants!

UNIT 11: HAVE A CONVERSATION AROUND DISTANCE CLASSROOM NORMS

In an age appropriate way, somewhere close to the first day, or even the very first day, have this conversation. Posting a list of class rules is simply not as effective and does not promote student agency or a learning community. Good teaching anywhere, and especially at a distance, involves students in decision making, goal setting, and community building--and that includes norms. I am specifically avoiding the word Rules. Rules are rigid things that require a consequence when broken, and they will be broken--by accident, on purpose by a student who doesn't agree with them, or a student who wants to test the teacher, or, or or....who needs it? Norms, by contrast, are agreed upon ways of doing things in the teaching space that contribute to a positive community. If you feel that you are releasing some of your control, that is OK to feel of course...in the end, the norms are still yours to approve or not. The difference is, through this process, you give the students a voice and student opinion is heard and thoughtfully considered.

Example: is eating allowed during class time? This is a hotly contested topic among distance educators. Perhaps in a classroom where eating and drinking occurred, some things to consider were the accumulation of trash, the possibility of attracting vermin, and spills that can become hazardous. All of these outcomes could have become school issues--but when students are in their own homes, are they learning concerns? Are they still distractions? Or, in some cases, do students need to eat /drink when they can due to other issues in the house, such as large families, limited space at the table, food insecurity? These are issues your students may or may not want to discuss, but as educators, these are things we need to consider.

Another example: dress code. This is also a hotly debated issue among distance teachers. These students, learning remotely, are in their own homes. Should they be in uniform, if your school has one? Should your students be required to wear shoes? Can your students wear pajamas? Lacking a policy from your school, the decision comes to you and your class. Have the conversation. Give your students a voice. Listen to their reasons. Students should also listen to opinions-- and really decide what is important to you in making your learning community. This could truly be a community building activity-- creating the norms of the class. Norms around dressing, scheduling, eating, how and when to communicate appropriately...making this your first project as a group can be an excellent first project, and make your class a place where students feel they have agency and belonging. Students will feel they are seen and heard, and that is the best way to start the school year.

- Discussing norms with your students, instead of telling them what the rules are, fosters ownership and community from the start
- Having a discussion around norms is a student centered activity where students feel heard and valued
- Having a discussion does *not* equal 'students make the rules,' rather they contribute their viewpoint to create the environment where they will spend time learning

UNIT 12: WHAT IF CLASS IS A MESS? IDEAS THAT WORK--EVEN THROUGH A LENS

What do you do if, despite all of the above, your class is a mess: Look. If you're reading this, you are a teacher, or an administrator, or have some connection to the school community. You know that *the best classroom management is a good lesson plan, as well as good preparation.* You also know that sometimes, you can be ultra-prepared, you have done everything you can do, and walk into class (or in this case, down the hall to your home workspace) ready to hit it out of the park--and for whatever reason, your plan flops. It happens to the best teachers.

1. Take a deep breath and remember you can't control another human, either in your physical classroom or on your computer screen. When the discord starts, employ some simple measures to reel the attention back in; with younger students "clap once if you hear my voice.....clap twice if you hear my voice....." or a countdown until it is silent usually works well. With older kids, the less forced control the better. This is where setting up community and student buy-in from the start thwarts much of this kind of trouble before it begins. When I taught in a love classroom and I

felt the students drifting, I stopped cold, mid sentence; I stared at my shoes until the students were 'shushing' each other. Then I continued like nothing had gone wrong.

2. Give yourself grace and your students compassion. They are struggling through this global situation as well. They are not at their best. Let this take your blood pressure down a notch or two before moving on.

3. Change gears if you really feel you are losing your group. In online learning there should never be too much lecture/speaking in one direction anyway; student centered learning means the attention shouldn't be ON the teacher long term, so 'getting it back' shouldn't often be a problem.

4. Call on a single student by name that you know has something positive to add to the discussion; students will more quickly turn their attention to the sound of a new voice than more of yours.

5. Start an assignment early (surprise!), like one of the writing prompts you will find in Part 3, or a group work/collaborative learning activity.

6. In quality remote teaching, there is little discussion of negative consequences. Back in 1999, Alfie Kohn wrote a book called "Punished by Rewards," asserting that punishment (or consequences, which in schools are often the same thing with two different names) and rewards are two sides of the same coin, and neither are effective at classroom management. SO this means, no star charts (for younger students), no color bars, no incentives (you'll get a prize for reading 100 books by winter break!), no 0s in the grade book for missing homework. Assume your class does not need an outside force to control them; you couldn't control them anyway. The difference is, in person, you had the illusion that you could. From your home office, can you force a student to log in? Press 'Submit Assignment'? Of course not. They will or they won't. If you have successfully built a community feel to your classroom from the start and put content on the back burner until it was in place, many

of these problems fix themselves; students want to show up for class. They want to feel like they are a part of something positive. They want to be in a successful community. Remember, they are isolated from their friends as well. Let them show up and use Flipgrid (a digital teaching tool that crosses education with video selfies, more on that later), and they won't want to miss it. And.....they are still the students, the younger ones, and they will still have silly, off days when they simply cannot keep it together. Resist the urge to get pulled into the power struggle and 'get them back.' Read the room, remember your 'Guide On The Side' status, and try corralling them into something productive. But no punishments. That will only fuel their fire.

UNIT 13: ALWAYS REMEMBER THE DISTANCE TEACHING BOUNCE BACK

Anything you can do, the students can do a (younger, more limited) version of as well. If you are teaching a lesson about literature, for example, when a poem moves in one direction and not another. Don't be afraid to *take* it in that direction and *bounce the issue back* to the students. "Why should the poem go this way?" Or perhaps you will have an especially creative writer in your group who will argue that it *shouldn't* have gone in that direction and back it up with an excellent reason. In math, purposely complete a problem incorrectly and say, "Why not?" to the class and have someone re-teach (bounce back) the concept to the group. Not only is teaching a higher order thinking skill demonstration for the students, the bounce back shows the teacher who understands the concept and who doesn't; it is an informal assessment of any lesson.

- The Bounce Back helps students and teachers alike
- The Bounce Back is an informal assessment
- The Bounce Back gives additional teaching for students who need it

UNIT 14: HOW TO END THE FIRST DISTANCE TEACHING DAY ON A BRIGHT NOTE

Ending the day with a slogan, a sign off, a cheer, a song, something the whole class does together binds your class even though they are learning remotely. This should be student generated and student led, and possibly rotated between students who want to create and lead it. Some ideas can come from long running TV shows or movies with many parts, usually in the sci-fi genre. The best sign offs and slogans have a hopeful message that works well to end the day with a positive, shared moment. One example is a shortened phrase from the Latin "Through adversity to the stars," and was featured in the movie Ad Astra, "To Infinity, and Beyond!" from Toy Story, and other call and response sayings, like "See you later, alligator....after a while, crocodile." "Remember, X days until Friday (or the next school break). Remember to keep your students' ages and content area in mind when choosing and guiding your students. A close friend showed his class the scene from the movie Dead Poets Society when Robin Williams explains why "Carpe Diem" is such an important phrase, and that phrase became his class' sign off. And, sticking with the student agency piece, solicit suggestions for creative and original sign offs from your students; they are often better connected to pop culture and will offer great ideas themselves.

HANDS ON APPROACH TO VIRTUAL TEACHING (PT 2)

UNIT 1: NOW WHAT? HERE IS WHAT COMES NEXT, DAY 2 AND MORE

You have survived your first day. Congratulations, that was no small task. Day 2, and onwards.....what you are being asked to do is monumental and we want to acknowledge that here. Teachers did not ask for this sudden, sweeping, all encompassing change in teaching paradigm; but this workbook is here to give you continuous, hands on, use-this-right-now guidance to get you through it.

In Part 1, building the community feeling in your classroom was the main focus of your opening days. Using the bonding activities, student agency and buy in, and student input in creating classroom norms and schedules were the important glue that helped in that creation. At this point, both you and your students have shared parts of yourself, had a good laugh or two, held up pictures (photos and original artwork), and generally connected with each other over the opening school days. You've made your class a place the students want to join, not a place students *must* log into, and that was the goal. Now, delivering the content becomes far less of a challenge, which is doubly terrific because delivering content online is a challenge when you have not been trained to do so in the first place. But read on. We are about to make it even easier for you, so you can concentrate on continuing the community building and keeping that connection alive, which only you can do in real time. Let's dive in together and look at the three basic tenets as you continue to build your learning environment.

- The next step after building engagement and connection in your classroom is delivering content
- Distance teaching changes the way content delivery happens
- Student centered learning is crucial in every lesson and every step going forward

UNIT 2: THE TRIPOD OF DISTANCE TEACHING

S tudent Centered Learning, Peer and Student/Teacher Relationships; and Quality Content with Real World Applications. Each of these really does put the learner in the center of the educational space, *as it always should have been* in a quality learning situation. This crisis citation has forced us to look at distance learning practices as *educational* practices, and we ask ourselves, *are we teaching this way because it is what we've always done? Or because it is the best way to do it?*

Student Centered Learning—of course the teacher knows more content than the student. That follows logically. That doesn't mean we all learn the same way, demonstrate mastery of content the same way, process information the same way at the same speed, etc. SO it makes sense that to stand in front of a room of 20-30 different personalities, even of the same or similar age, and lecture to them and expect them all to learn it the same way, is laughable. This realization is starting to dawn on the people who run educational systems. If we as educators, the ones in the trenches, put students in the center of the process, and address the learning styles and differences, we improve the entire system. **The more students can be at the center of the learning process, the better the process becomes.**

Peer and Student/Teacher Relationships--we talked about spending a great deal of class time in the opening days (weeks?) creating a community in your digital classroom. If you teach an elementary grade, you were going strong all day with the same group. If you teach older students, you started again several times a day with a new group and probably felt a slightly different dynamic with each group. That is ok. I imagine that dynamic will change as the year rolls along. There will be students who do not want to buy into being part of a community and I advise you to keep reaching out. You never know when or how you will make a difference to that student.

Quality Content with Real World Applications--whatever your content area, quality content is important no matter what the setting. Long gone are the days of lecture, hand out a worksheet, review worksheet, class dismissed. Quality content demands real world applications, so no matter what your subject area is (or in the case of elementary teaching, what subject you are teaching in the moment), relating that content back to the everyday lives of the students is crucial for connection. And connection is crucial for quality distance learning.

Really, if you look closely, all of these three return to student centered learning. Distance teaching puts students at the center. Everyday.

- The tenets of distance teaching are student centered learning, peer to teacher relationships, and real world connections to content
- Content moves closer to the forefront as we move away form the opening days of school, but relationships remain important throughout the year
- Always connect content to real world situations beyond your classroom

UNIT 3: HOW TO SHIFT YOUR PLANS TO BE REMOTE, EFFICIENT, AND STUDENT CENTERED

The pandemic, and subsequent shift to distance teaching, has uncovered many outdated teaching practices that should have been abandoned long ago in *any* setting. Even in brick and mortar classrooms, the talking head 'expert' in the front of the room doing chalk and talk lessons (which we'd hoped had been abandoned long ago!) has mostly moved to the Guide On The Side. I've observed teachers who have been in the field for 40+ years hanging onto the perceived control they have of their class when they are always talking, always giving notes, handing out test after test. Any expert in his or her field could (get over their fear of public speaking and) do the same thing. Teaching and talking are not the same. Teaching in any setting involves varied and engaging activities that address multiple learning styles and, sometimes, learning differences. In remote learning scenarios, the best online teachers do as little talking/lecturing as possible. Online teachers give minimal, necessary information on a new topic, usually introduced with a real world hook ("You know what happened to me yesterday? I was trying to figure out how to cross that really busy street down by.....and the cars were moving at......."). Then some examples might follow, an informal check for understanding and a solicitation for questions. A note about questions: WAIT. It is common that teachers do not give enough wait time when asking a question, especially in online learning, because everyone staring at a screen becomes awkward. It's true, and that's OK. The more you do it, the less awkward it becomes. Plus, the seat time simply does not translate minute for minute. Now, the teacher only presents only the basic information students need, then steps aside, and sees where they can synthesize the missing pieces. Good online instructors ask leading questions. Structure your lessons to have short teacher led time and LONG student work time, where you can check in one by one.

To make the real shift start to student centered learning, distance learning teachers start by giving the class the large, overarching themes of the content you are teaching. The big ideas. The lightbulb moments. The information you are sure they came to you not knowing, or not understanding fully. Figuring out these big pieces, these effective starting points can come through entrance tickets, (What happened in America right after the Civil War? State three things you remember from last year./ What is the Pythagorean theorem?/What is the most important rule of football and why?), a simple conversation, or just diving right in. Frame the content on these larger chunks of basic information. Simplify the central idea of the lesson, keep that concrete and technical, and then turn to some essential questions; these tend to be open ended, multi-answered questions that stimulate conversation, more questions, and encourage a deeper understanding of the original concept. It is *here* where the lesson moves from teacher to student centered. Of course the teacher needs to give the main idea, concept, formula, factual part of the lesson; from there, introduce the essential questions and you'll hear more from the students. Allow students to answer each other and *guide* answers that seem to be getting off track. This is where your guide on the side role kicks in.

Here are some examples of content area and essential questions:

- Music: How did the city where Beethoven composed

influence what he composed? How does the community you live in influence the music you choose?

- Math: When is a time/where is a place when we do not want to choose the 'best' answer? Is there a math problem where there is no 'best answer?
- Art: How does the culture of an artists' home country affect the art s/he creates?
- English: what devices do authors use to keep their readers from putting their books down? Why do you personally keep reading?
- Geography: How do the land and water features in your community affect how you live your daily lives?
- Science: How does science affect your daily life today?

This style of student centered learning will lead to deeper understanding of bigger ideas, and will also increase your students' ability to process information independently.

When assigning student centered, authentic assessments, keep these essential questions in mind. Notice that each of these examples has the words 'we' or 'your' in them? That's not an accident.

- In distance teaching, your role changes from talking head to Guide On The Side
- Students are always in the center of learning; present the big ideas and essential questions and give students the room to connect the dots
- Cooperative learning activities are a great way to transition from the teacher led part of the lesson to the demonstration of mastery
- Keep teacher centered learning time to a minimum
- Distance learning educators should not try to give the students all the information on a topic or unit; in remote, online learning, teachers give the overarching, big ideas and ask essential questions, and allow the students to ask

probing questions and do research on their own and in cooperative groups to dig deeper and to find answers

- Seat time in online learning does not transfer from traditional teaching 1:1; when done well, distance learning should take less 'in class' time

UNIT 4: SAMPLE DISTANCE TEACHING LESSON PLAN TEMPLATES

Below you will find some easily edited sample lesson plans that work well in the remote classroom.

Day/Date/Letter

Topic/Unit

Objectives

1. **What** are students learning?
2. **Why** are they learning it?
3. **How** can they demonstrate mastery of learning?
4. **How** will students stay connected to each other?
5. **What** SEL is included?

Focus Activity:

Content:
    Synchronous--in class:

Asynchronous--out of class:

Resources:

Closing:
    Assessment (formal/informal)
    Reflection Activity
    Reminders?
    Next Steps....

Filled out, this template might look like this for my high school music class:

Day/Date/Letter: Monday, Sept. 14, 2020/Day C

Topic/Unit/Essential Question:: Music History, Hildegard of Bingen: How did women influence music before the 1400s?

Objectives:
    What are students learning?
    The life of composer Hildegard, her music, her writings, her recipes, her music modernized

Why are they learning it?

To show how 12th century music can connect to today's music

How can they demonstrate mastery of learning?

Exit tickets with 3 new pieces of information

How will students stay connected to each other?

During the listening examples, encourage students to ask each other for opinions and comparisons. What does Hildegard's music sound similar to?

What SEL is included? Poetry in Motion: write a poem about your morning, like Hildegard did

Focus Activity: Listening Example--"Vision," by Hildegard

Content:

Synchronous--in class: quick listening example, quick bio, show images; turn and talk activity; story of Richard Souther and updated world music, new Listening Example

Asynchronous--out of class: look up one of Hildegard's 'recipes' and tell the class tomorrow why it is still useful 8 centuries later!

Resources: Hildegard YouTube videos, images, Hildegard poetry.

Closing:

Assessment (formal/informal): Exit ticket with 3 pieces of information learned that wasn't known before class

Reflection Activity--if you were to write a play of your life, as Hildegard did, what would the title be?

Reminders? None today.

Next Steps....On to Gregorian Chant in Europe.

Or, the filled out lesson plan might look like this for an elementary math class:

Day/Date/Letter--Monday , September 14, 2020 (Day E)

Topic/Unit/Essential Question--Math, the number 6: How is number six important to you?

Objectives:

What are students learning? The properties of 6; numbers that add to 6, objects that represent 6

Why are they learning it? Symbols that represent items is a basic math property, encourages counting skills

How can they demonstrate mastery of learning? Students will hold up a filled out paper at the end of class

How will students stay connected to each other? Assign students numbers 1-6; break in lesson to do an impromptu 'count off'/ Raise your hand if you are a 3/6/1/2...../hold up 6 fingers

What SEL is included? Students will choose their favorite emoji and draw it 6 times.

Focus Activity: show the video "The Number Six" from YouTube, by StoryBots, NetflixJr

Content:

Synchronous--in class: review counting 1-5, ask various students to collect 1, 2, 3, 4, 5, of different objects; practice writing 6; students choose an object to draw 6 times (shapes, faces, houses, cakes, etc); introduce number trees that show 6+0, 5+1, etc.

On their own: Draw five different items six times; draw a rainbow with any six colors

Asynchronous--out of class: Practice drawing 6, practice writing 1, 2, 3, 4, 5, 6 three times

Resources: YouTube, NetflixJr., WhiteBoard and Markers

Closing:

Assessment (formal/informal)--Addition problems made by students for each other to answer, using numbers 1-6

Reflection Activity--what was difficult about this lesson? What was simple? What should I repeat?

Reminders? Cut out #7 and decorate to post tomorrow

Next Steps....tomorrow we introduce 7. What do we already know about #7? What can you guess about 7?

. . .

As you can see from these templates, the *content section is significantly shorter* than the objectives and the closing; that is because in distance learning, the content routinely takes a backseat to connections; between the students and teachers, and between the subject and the real world. You are an expert on your content, you've spent years studying it and possibly teaching it; concentrate now on the delivery and the connections, and making sure your students feel like they are a part of a community and what you are teaching is important in their worlds beyond the classroom. This difference in teaching style is reflected very clearly in how these templates are laid out. The entrance and the exit is at least as, if not more important than the content.

- In distance teaching, relationships are at least as important as content, early on relationships are *more* important than content
- SEL needs to be included in every lesson plan
- Demonstration of mastery must be clearly stated in each plan
- Always know your next steps
- Include student connections in every lesson

UNIT 5: LONG TERM REMOTE PLANNING, WITH EXAMPLES

W hat do you want them to be able to do at the end of your course? If you teach elementary school, what are the goals for your grade? If you teach high school, how can students demonstrate mastery to you?

As an example, I was trained as a music teacher in 1995. To say we were amongst the first group of teachers to have authentic assessments would be an understatement—we were using authentic assessments in front of an audience of community members before the term was in use. Each summer, music teachers poured through dozens of scores and decided to build our programs based on our instrumentation, our musical goals, the playing level of our students, and other criteria, creating a balanced performance—but we *always* started at the end. The product. The *demonstration of mastery* of the piece. Then we worked backwards to figure out how the students could meet that goal. Some questions we were trained to ask while planning were: where are the pitfalls? Which instruments have the melody, the harmony, with which other sections, and where? For how long? Where is it essential for students to mark their breaths and page turns?

Let's look at this example through the distance learning lens: there is a musical score. I understand it beginning to end, because I am the studied expert. Could I lecture about it and tell every student what to do and how to do it? Sure. But that is *not* the best way to *teach*. I give students their parts. Those are those are the big ideas: the key signatures, the note ranges, the patterns. Then I ask the students to move into their instrument groups (cooperative learning, turn and talk). Together they locate long playing areas that will require breath support while marking their parts with breath reminders; they identify repeated patterns to break up practicing (If page 4 and page 8 are the same, they don't need to be practiced twice); find places where the group part matches another group part (changing the groups in cooperative learning), locate especially different passages and discuss which techniques will best be useful. In fifteen minutes, we come together as a class to create a 'mind map' of the piece (using a digital format for increased engagement) with everyone's ideas so we have a visual representation of the piece from beginning to end.

Will the students learn the piece better with this sort of preparation than a lecture, even if they are interested enough in the music to take notes? 100% yes. When I added interesting stories about the composer (there are always interesting stories about composers, they are a crazy group of people!), creating liner notes about where and when the music had been performed in the past, and immediately the students are more than performers, they are pulled into the piece, *at the center* not only of the music but of the lesson and the entire unit.

This is how I would plan every lesson to go everyday in my brick and mortar classroom--after I was trained to be an online educator, so it is easy to see how these techniques transfer to the digital space.

"Demonstrate/demonstration of mastery" is a very important phrase in distance learning. Coupled with student centered learning, it is what distance learning is all about. Clear away anything extra, any 'fluff' activities. What do you want your students to do later that they can't do now, and how can they show you that they've learned to do it? *That* is the big question. Start with that question for every unit. Then determine how they can show you--traditional test? Essay? Maybe. But there are so many more digital assessments out there students can use now--FlipGrid, Seesaw, Screencastify, PreziNext....the list is long and varied, and gives students many ways to show you they 'get it.' Some students may want to write a story or poem. Some will write a script—and cast it, shoot it, and allow you to see it. Let their creativity lead them to show you that they can demonstrate understanding *their* way. This will accommodate learning differences and styles, and keep your classroom feeling more like a community with student centered learning taking the lead. Plus, creating the assessment (and in the best case, a rubric with it), shows a very high level of engagement and agency in your class; this is a tremendous win for the teacher. This kind of learning inspires life long memories of your subject and positive experiences in your class.

- Student centered learning often incorporates turn and talk activities, culminating with a large group sharing of ideas
- The student activity portion of the lesson should be longer than the teacher led portion, generally
- Rubrics will give students a complete understanding of what is expected in a project, and creates transparency in assessments

UNIT 6: DIGITAL OPTIONS FOR DEMONSTRATING MASTERY, EXPLAINED

G oogle Classroom: This seems to be the Standard Bearer for many districts moving to an all online format in the wake of the global pandemic. Google Classroom has actually been around long before thousands of districts really needed it to be; I was using Google Classroom and Blackboard as 'back up' plan books and places to post assignments for students who had been absent to grab what they missed. It was a great place to store important documents digitally and start saving the trees. Students as well as parents were then able to access any of my many important communications day or night. Snow days took on a whole new meaning, as administrators began to grasp that with the Internet, snow days were not *lost* days any longer--and they didn't need to be made up, either. Finally the school calendar had a firm end date!

Here is the other side of that coin, though Google Classroom can be used alone, it was never *meant* to be used alone. Perhaps for the elementary grades it is sufficient, but for middle and high school students who need a more immersive, interactive experience, Google Classroom was only meant to be a piece of the Google Suite--not the entire experience. If you are using the other parts of the suite, like Google Meet, Google Slides, Sheets, Hangouts, Podcasts, Docs, and

Collections, great. But if you're ready to expand your arsenal, here are some great new products you can start using to help create a student centered, community based classroom:

FlipGrid: picture an educational short form, entertaining video format where students can respond (in selfie video form) to a question posed by a teacher. The question could be something like, "What do you think life on Mars is like?," coming after a short paragraph of the conditions that exist on Mars. Each 'comment' is a twenty second video selfie of a student recording his or her own answer with a device, and each student in class can see it and respond to it. Students can see each other, respond to
     each other, pose questions directly to each other....you've created an (almost) in person conversation.

Seesaw: Seesaw is a digital portfolio platform for grades K-12. Students can 'show what they know,' an important phrase in student centered learning. We want students to be able to demonstrate mastery of their concepts in the best way for *the student*, and Seesaw allows students many outlets for demonstration. They can upload pictures and videos, PDFs, text based documents, drawings, and links, and everything is sharable with other students and families with teacher approval. According to Seesaw's own efficacy study, 80% of participating teachers saved 3 hours or more per week on tasks like grading, parents communication, and sending school reports, because Seesaw was able to streamline this so efficiently. 80% of teachers reported that Seesaw helped them stay in contact with parents and families that were difficult to reach before they started using Seesaw.

PearDeck: This new slides based presentation software will integrate with existing Google Slides OR PowerPoint presentations, AND it adds the engagement piece for every student. Each Pear Deck slide invites students to interact with your presentation from their screen.

First, your students 'join' your deck with a code (similar to Google Classroom) and they can view your Slides or PowerPoint as usual.....when a PearDeck slide appears, it will have a question or prompt. Once students answer, the teacher can make all responses visible but anonymous, or put names to answers. This piece of software is flexible, user friendly, and applicable to every subject area. Teachers simply use the PearDeck add-on to their Google accounts. Additionally, you can create an entire presentation only using PearDeck. Super simple.

Screencastify: This is a Chrome extension (a piece of software that 'lives' within the Chrome browser on your computer, you simply follow prompts to put it there) that allows teachers to make recordings up to five minutes long (in the free version) and save them to their Google Drive or upload to a private YouTube account for later use. Teachers can explain complicated subjects, recap the day, or record morning introductions with this software. User support gets five stars according to Common Sense Education. This product is recommended for grades 3-12 only.

Prezi Next: I was a Prezi user years ago, when studying for my Distance Learning certificate, and Prezi (now called Prezi Next) has gone through many changes and improvements since. This is presentation software with two major differences that allow it to stand out from Google Slides, Pear Deck, and PowerPoint: The presentation starts with an overview of every slide, zoomed way out; and each transition zooms out and back in, similarly to globe trotting on Google Earth. This creates a 3D, travel sensation that brings back any wandering minds in your virtual classroom. The suggestion of movement is more engaging than other presentation software. Beyond that, Prezi Next has no other bells or whistles to complete with PowerPoint or Google Slides.

. . .

Venngage: This website is free for educators and students, and offers customizable templates based on the kind of work you do. Although a pay version is available with more templates, the free version offers more than a dozen colorful templates that are perfect for visual learners to organize information and present it in a static way. Venngage has mind maps, flow charts, timelines, diagrams, resumes, and poster templates that are all fully customizable for any subject. Students can log in with an email or school account. Venngage has been referred to as the 'best kept secret in the digital classroom' for its user friendliness and wide variety of free templates. Users have gone so far as to say it is 'professional grade' and are wowed by the ability to upload your own pictures for content. Being able to personalize and bring your own life into your assignments can be very important for your students in distance learning; always strive to include real world connections wherever possible.

Artsonia: I would be remiss if I did not include at least one related arts digital platform. Artsonia, while not new, is an online portfolio, a kind of digital museum, and your students are the curators. Students can show off their work, comment on each other's masterpieces, and let visitors know when new pieces have been installed. There is also space for student reflection on their work, a very important part of the National Standards for the Arts.

Visme: this is a presentation software whose functionality is 80% free, with no limits. Several students and adults using Visme for business get Visme "Zero downsides" because of its user friendly interface and "the feeling like you're a kid in a candy store." Infographics including time-lines, calendars, workflow charts, presentations and flyers are only some of the creatable available on the free version of Visme. This is a great tool for both the teacher AND the student in the distance education setting. The visuals are engaging without being flashy.

UNIT 7: HOW TO GIVE AND RECEIVE FEEDBACK IN THE DIGITAL SPACE

F requent, formal and non formal feedback is essential during distance teaching. The everyday interactions, the small, seemingly inconsequential interactions teachers had in the same physical space with students daily result in communication are suddenly gone in distance teaching. We now know these moments were *not* inconsequential. These moments of connection and communications are crucial for student success, and when students learn at a distance the teacher needs to be proactive about replacing those lost moments. From the quick "Excellent response," "Nice work," "Great job," to the longer, more thought out written responses to formal unit assessments and projects, distance learning thrives on almost constant feedback. Positive feedback builds upon itself, like putting gas in a car; picture your students rolling down the highway, but every so often, no matter how great the weather or driving conditions, they are going to need a 'fill up' from you. Positive feedback, even a small amount, can rescue a student from loneliness and isolation. Feedback means the student is seen. When needed, your re-direction is best received when it is delivered with a smile in a helpful tone, always with the desire to see your students be as successful as possible. No matter what age they are, students sometimes need to hear just that.

Giving feedback to your students can come in the form of email, phone calls, texts, and as comments on formal assessments.

Getting feedback from the students is equally important. I could never imagine looking out at a class in a brick and mortar class room and asking, "So, how do you think I am doing?" but this is just another example of how distance learning is --and should be-- different from face to face experiences.

(Also, I would never ask that particular question. I'm teaching, not doing stand up at the Laugh Factory.)

Instead, focused, age appropriate questions to the students can inform your teaching as you move through the school year.

1. Can you easily find what you need in the digital classroom?
2. Have you had technical issues, such as sound or slow load time, and do you know how to report those issues?
3. Are my lessons, assignments, and due dates clear to you?
4. Do you feel comfortable asking questions?
5. Do you feel like you're being heard in this class?
6. How would you improve this distance learning experience?

Not every question needs to be asked of every student everyday. But just as feedback is valuable and more than that, necessary, for your students' improvement, it is necessary for you to improve as a distance educator. Remember that feedback in general needs to be *timely* and *actionable*. While a student might like to hear "Great job!," but there is nothing actionable there. Be specific, tell them what went well and what can be better next time. No one gets everything 100% right every time. Not even the teacher. Feedback can be asked and answered in the form of email, text, or added onto assessments for no point value. Feedback can also be part of a morning meeting or a casual conversation; as long as it is happening in varied and purposeful ways, both to and from you and your students.

UNIT 8: HOW TO CREATE AUTHENTIC ASSESSMENTS WHILE TEACHING ONLINE

Informal assessments should be an ongoing process while distance teaching, and that can be as quick as answering a simple question or correcting a student's misunderstanding of a concept. Informal assessment can also be students submitting an exit ticket (digitally, or with pen and paper held up to the screen) with 1-5 pieces of information they learned that day. Allow them to write any pieces of information they have leaving class that they did not have when they entered. That will be a physical indication of what stuck and what did not. If you thought a big idea was taught and not one student wrote that on an exit ticket, chances are the idea was lost somewhere in translation and you will want to circle back to that.

Another example of an informal assessment: students create a quiz to give to another student in class. Let the students grade each other with comments, and then you look over the results. This works well with older students; younger ones can talk about concepts with each other and then write one or two examples of what their partner did well.

Students of all ages can participate in a speed round of age appropriate popcorn questions, which easily translates from the physical classroom to Google Meet or Zoom: each student prepares a question about the topic or lesson in advance, and the teacher calls on the first student to read his/her question and call on another student to answer. That student then asks his/her question and calls on another student to answer, and so on until all questions have been asked. If a student doesn't know an answer, the teacher can step in to keep things moving.

The information you receive from ongoing informal assessment is helpful in two ways: one, it shows if your students are receiving the information you are hoping they retain, and two, if any one or two students in particular are struggling and falling behind. If this kind of ongoing assessment is happening quickly and informally every or every other day, you can catch this before the train has completely jumped the track.

If you complete an ongoing string of informal assessments, formal assessment should not be the 'dark cloud on the horizon' event it was when I was in public school (it was the Carter Administration). Back then there were two main kinds of formal assessments that determined a large chunk of your class grade: tests and papers. Not a good test taker? Not a good writer? For the most part, your grades were never that good. Thank goodness we have evolved past that. Mostly.

In distance teaching, giving students agency in your classroom community applies to formal assessment as well. With all the choices in the digital space, students can demonstrate mastery of concepts in many different ways. This isn't to say a student *must always* use digital media for formal assessment. Sometimes students do prefer exams and essays, and sometimes teachers prefer to assign them. They are not inherently bad, they only need to be structured to demonstrate higher thinking skills. If students are only memorizing facts and figures for an exam, that is not learning. If students are using higher order thinking (see chart below), we have evidence of long term learning.

LOTS (lower order thinking skills)   HOTS (higher order thinking skills)

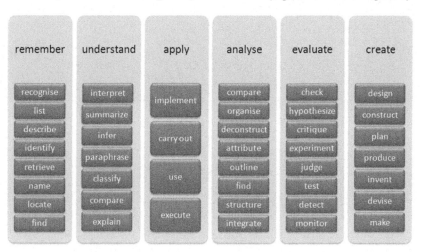

Demonstration of mastery requires **HOTS (Higher Order Thinking Skills)**, across all grades. A look at that in a math class, for example, might look like this:

- *Concepts taught in isolation, like equations VS. Real world applications of the concept*
- *Rote, repetitive problems to use class time VS. Moving on--seat time is not mastery*
- *Right/Wrong answer based VS. Students listing ways these concepts apply to their lives*
- *Passive student note taking VS. Questioning, rearranging problems, 'what if' situations*
- *Units taught in separation VS. Students making connections between concepts*

What High Order Thinking Skills, especially important in a student centered, distance learning classroom, are used here? Hypothesizing, critiquing, constructing, designing, and planning, to start. When you can use those HOTS verbs to describe your lesson plans and formal assessments, you know you are making learning student centered and masterful.

UNIT 9: THE BEST WAYS TO GET PARENTS INVOLVED IN YOUR VIRTUAL CLASSROOM

Having parents involved and informed is crucial. There are many creative ways to accomplish this. One very basic way is to make your contact information easily accessible in your online classroom, everyday. It should be front and center, with a live link to your email. Make the most useful contact known. On a regular basis, at least bi-monthly, share information about what your class is doing on a curricular and non-curricular level with parents. There are many activities that can involve parents, even if that means logging in after hours.

1. Get to know the parents and let the parents get to know you. Ask parents if they want to participate in their own 'get to know you' event or list, where they can contact each other if they have a question about class or want to participate in creating a parents group to support the learning in your class.

2. Perhaps one of the parents has a hidden talent they can share--maybe a parent can create a newsletter to inform the parents about the class? Maybe another has IT chops to help out when there are computer problems?

3. Stay in touch with your parents and let them know you have

an Open Door policy. You can set aside office hours for parents by appointment only.

4. Have a cultural awareness event (in lieu of a cultural potluck dinner or fashion show) where parents can log on with their students to share pictures or literature from their culture.

5. Another idea is to send updates to parents via Snail Mail or an actual telephone call. Parents will appreciate that you took time out of your day to touch base with them and talk to them about their child, your student, about more than their grades and achievements. I know you're busy. Maybe doing this once every few days makes the juice worth the squeeze.

6. Use the Remind app (or another like it) to send out quick notes to parents about upcoming events and assessments. You can make distribution lists within the app that include your students as well.

7. If it takes a village to raise a child, it takes a group of parents to make a class of online learners successful. Just a handful of parents can come together to create a Parent Club (with a better name) to support your efforts and the students' efforts. Include the idea for that organization in the first communication home at the start of the school year. All hands on deck, they say at sea.

UNIT 10: WRITING PROMPTS FOR QUIET MOMENTS IN DISTANCE LEARNING

Across all content areas, writing skills are being stressed now more than ever before. In the distance teaching space, using a writing prompt is a great way to create a student centered activity while continuing to build community and student teacher relationships. You can extend the activity by inviting students to share their writing or allowing them to keep their writing private. Using a digital journal (like Google Blog) is an easy way to capture this type of work on an ongoing basis in the digital space.

Here are twenty writing prompts you can use or modify for your students. Remember to keep the prompts age and content area appropriate, and set a minimum number of acceptable sentences:

- An assignment I wish you would give is...
- The hardest test/project I ever completed was...
- The worst birthday I ever had was...
- The best present I ever received was...
- The best song lyric I ever heard was...
- The greatest movie ever is...
- If I won the lottery I would...
- The coolest place I ever visited was...

- Something I learned this year that I still can't believe is...
- If I could be anywhere right now it would be...
- An idea I have for an app is...
- A device/appliance/piece of furniture I had in my home is...
- Right now I would rather be doing/traveling to...
- After high school I want to...
- The most awesome relative I have is...
- My favorite ice cream/pizza topping is...
- If I could paint my house any color it would be...
- The greatest scent is...
- My favorite piece of art is...
- My favorite video game as a child was...

HANDS ON APPROACH TO VIRTUAL TEACHING (PT 3)

UNIT 1: DISTANCE TEACHING BEYOND DAY 2, WEEK 1, AND ONTO THE SEMESTER

As you take a step back and catch your breath after days one and two, really 'zoom out' and see the calendar in the monthly view. Then the semester. This is a marathon, not a sprint. In general, the first week (five school days) are spent on connection, community building, and engagement. Usually school does not start on a Monday, so there will be a weekend in there to break that up. One major goal would be to commit every name to memory, that shows the students that you are committed to creating a community; you are more than a giver of assignments and grades. Another would be to be able to connect one fact about that student, beyond their name, to the student. After six days, if you truly have been focused on community building and student engagement activities, the proof would be in looking at any face in your class and being able to say to yourself, "That is Robert. He has a little sister." The fact you associate with your student this early on does not have to be something deep or serious; a single basic fact at this point is a win.

Around the start of the sixth day, slowly, effective distance teachers begin bringing in content. Normally this starts with a class outline or syllabus, whichever is more appropriate for the grade you teach. Reviewing this document (or presenting it digitally, preferably) is a teacher led activity, so remember to bookend it with student centered activities. Each day going forward should introduce more of the content in steady increments. *But always remember engagement and community is of equal importance to content.*

Be careful not to rush through your outline or syllabus. It is here that your expectations are first stated. Clear and consistent expectations are very important, considering that this online environment removes the casual, incidental contact where students can ask for clarification.

- The first five or six days of school are usually broken up by a weekend, giving you and your students a break in your opening week plans
- The time you spend learning names and something more about your students is critical to building trusting relationships in your classroom
- Add content slowly, starting with an outline or syllabus, but do not abandon the activities that build community
- Remember to keep teacher centered time limited to presenting the big ideas and essential questions of your topic

UNIT 2: HOW TO ADD SOCIAL EMOTIONAL LEARNING IN THE ONLINE CLASSROOM

Social Emotional Learning Activities will work well in the distance teaching space. I worked in a high school for years where the first experience of the day was called CPR (Connecting, emPowering, Revitalizing). This 20 minute block was dedicated time for students to have a 'soft landing' into the environment for learning. Twenty minutes may be too long a period of time to spend in your learning space, but even ten minutes daily to address SEL is important. Try an SEL activity to bond your group and set a positive mood in your class.

1. Ask students to think of three words, which can be related to answer this question: How are you today? On the board behind you, or even on a piece of paper you hold on the screen, you can have words in columns or color coded from which the students can choose: simpler emotions for younger students, more complex for older students. They then write the words that best express how they are. Simple. The point is, someone is asking them, they know someone wants to know. For many students, **showing up for school is motivated by the need to be seen** and heard; knowing

this is one of the first things you may do will encourage students to engage in your daily activities. You are showing your students you see them and want to hear from them. That is the first step to really knowing them, an essential part of connecting in distance learning.

2. From the amazing Social Emotional Learning and Growth Mindset resources provided by stormprogram.com. Descriptions and links are provided at the end of this book.

3. Pizza Man (modified Hangman): using a smaller SEL word like "kind" for lower elementary, "thoughtful" for upper elementary and middle school grades, and a short sentence like "I am thoughtful" for high school, draw the dashed lines on the board behind you for the letters, a smiley face for the "Pizza Man," and a big, round, pizza cut into 8 slices. Each time a letter is guessed, it is either added to the word/phrase or if it is not in the word/phrase, a pizza slice is shaded. If the word/phrase is revealed before all the pizza is eaten, the whole class wins. Once all letters are revealed, challenge younger students to use the word in a sentence; ask older students how they can be thoughtful in an *active* way for the rest of the day.

4. Wisdom Wednesday: this is when the SEL activities can revolve around a deep thinking question. In pairs, possibly in breakout rooms, private Zoom calls, or for older students, text, students can answer the question, "What does caring/giving/sharing mean to you?" Older students can then extend their answer to include hypothetical and real life examples.

5. Emotion Detectives: the teacher secretly sends an emotion word to a student. That student tells the class a story of a time when s/he experienced that emotion, but cannot use the emotion word. After 30 seconds, the class has to guess the word.

6. Reflection Fridays: Mindfulness is getting a lot of attention these days and for good reason--clearing out your thoughts and simply focusing on your breathing and being in the

moment is beneficial for your mental and physical health. This activity may need small tweaks to be age appropriate for all grades, but in general is a great activity for all grades. Ask your students to sit cross legged on their chairs, with a straight back. Eyes can be opened or closed. Put on some soft, mindfulness music (easily found online). Begin by telling the students to wrap their arms around themselves and give themselves a gentle hug. Next, read this narration while students slowly inhale and exhale: "Breathe in through your nose, breathe out through your mouth...feel the air enter your nose, feel it leave through your mouth, feel your chest rise, feel it fall back down. Because you care. Pick one other part of your body, and focus on how it feels. We will take 3 more slow breaths on my count ...1... 2... 3... Open your eyes." Then, take two student responses for each of these two reflection questions: Look around at your class. How do you think they feel right now? How can you tell what they are feeling?

UNIT 3: REAL LIFE STORIES FROM TEACHING ONLINE: WHAT WORKED, WHAT DIDN'T

In the spring of 2020, as distance teaching increased millions-fold, I was in close touch with many teachers who had to make the sudden change from the brick and mortar classroom to the remote teaching model. I frequently asked, what always worked for you, and what always crashed and burned? Here are some of the stories, used anonymously and with permission form these teachers, for your benefit:

- A 32 year old elementary school teacher told me that the turning point in her classroom came when she started 1:1 check ins. When she said 'turning point,' I asked for specifics. "Everything changed," she said. "Logging in on time. Engagement. Completing classwork and homework. Participating in cooperative learning. All I did was call homes, or email students and parents to say hello, ask how everyone was feeling, and have a two minute conversation about anything *but* academics. It was like magic.
- A 45 year old science teacher told me that if he could go back and 'redo' spring 2020, he would let go of classroom management issues like "turn on your camera!" and "Why

are you logging on late?" He said he had read about the importance of engagement and forging relationships with his students but clung so tightly to his content and curricula and *getting through the textbook,* that he, and I quote, "lost all of them. I lost all of the students. Their grades dropped, and the lower they dropped, the more I clung to the science curriculum. I tried to penalize students when they missed deadlines instead of asking them why assignments were late; I wish I hadn't been afraid to trust them more. What I feared the most is actually what happened. The harder I tried, the worse everything got, for everyone.

- A 28 year old art teacher thought the shift to online teaching would be simple for her content area; she actually felt pretty comfortable posting videos of herself teaching the lesson and demonstrating how to complete the art project from the start. However, when student work didn't come back, and parents emailed her to say they were so overwhelmed and their students were only completing the 'real' class work, she disengaged completely. She stopped posting assignments altogether and started looking for other work. In effect, she quit. "I regret that decision now," she says. "I wish I had realized that everyone was overwhelmed. I shouldn't have taken those emails so personally. I learned my lesson and now I am trying to get back into teaching.

- A 50 year old teacher who was participating in a 'reverse distance teaching' scenario reported how difficult it was to have distance learners in addition to students reporting to class on a hybrid schedule while she was teaching from home. The mixed environments definitely had an impact on the student learning. "I am trying to use as many distance teaching tools as possible, because I am remote, which kind of makes all of my learners remote, but the ones reporting to school (with a teacher aid for classroom management) are a distraction, and actually my distance learners are doing much better than the students reporting to school. Maybe

distance learning techniques should be taught to all
teachers."

- "All things being equal, I prefer distance teaching," reported
  a teacher in her 30s. "It sounds counter intuitive, but if you
  make the lessons student centered, the management piece
  falls into place on its own. I was reluctant to try it. I liked
  feeling in control. But this way definitely works better
  for me."
- "I realized my students paid more attention to my teacher
  time when I started by talking about something that had
  nothing to do with school," said a teacher in her 40s. "Once,
  I realized my desk was void of pictures of my family, which
  was different from how it looked when I was teaching in
  person. I slowly added pictures and started my days telling
  the stories behind each picture. Some were taken on family
  vacations, some were of my pets or family members, and a
  few were actually of me when I was young. My students
  were mesmerized. I had no idea how engaging this simple
  activity would be."

UNIT 4: CURRENT "OTHER" ISSUES IN DISTANCE TEACHING: PETS, SHOES, AND PJS, TOO

There is a growing, ever more interesting body of discussion around the etiquette of students participating in distance learning. As a distance teacher, you should be aware of these topics and decide where you stand on them, should they come up in your class.

- Students of all ages are 'bringing' their pets to class. In some cases, students are sitting in a common area of the house and if you've ever owned a pet, you know they go where they go. Overly affectionate dogs and hungry cats can be loud, distracting, and derail a class in about ten seconds. Some distance learning teachers are trying to 'ban' animals during class. I am not certain how they think they can accomplish this. I think it is important to remember that this is a big difference between traditional teaching and distance teaching--you, as the teacher, are entering the students' *homes*. Something to consider: do you think you can tell them where to sit and who can or cannot walk by? There is no right or wrong answer. It is something educators have to consider now that we never had to consider before.
- There is a charter school in Florida that has a dress code.

When it moved to distance learning in the spring of 2020, it still required students to adhere to the dress code---right down to the navy socks and brown loafers, that were never seen on the screen. I am certain there are many other schools that can tell the same story; if you are in control of this decision, what will you decide? Is footwear an important part of your classroom culture? Again, there is not a right or wrong answer. Every school, teacher, student, state, environment, is different. This is something to have on your radar, should you have to make the decision. Some teachers are saying to bicker over footwear that goes unseen in distance learning is a silly waste of time; others say being in school uniform from head to toe has a psychological effect on the student and puts them in a mind space for learning.

- Even farther out on the spectrum of school uniforms and acceptable attire is the topic of students wearing PJs on camera. Believe it or not, this is being debated by distance educators. Some argue that they want students to be comfortable, cozy, feel safe, and 'at home' metaphorically speaking. These teachers say the comfort level leads to decreased tardiness (no need for primping) and increased engagement, because students are completely relaxed, without worrying about their outfits. Other teachers are concerned that the lack of 'putting themselves together' will mentally keep students in a state of vacation brain. This is another case of 'know your students.' Know how they will best engage, interact, and relate to each other and you.

- Camera on/camera off? A seasoned distance learning educator recently asked for opinions about a student he says is engaged in chat, breakout rooms, and asks questions (in text formats) when she needs extra help. Her comments further class conversation (in text format only) and are thoughtful and resourceful. She helps her peers, turns in assignments on time, and her projects are top notch. But, she refuses to turn on her camera or her microphone. If this student's engagement is evident everywhere else, is it a requirement that her camera and microphone are on? As the teacher, you may be the one to prioritize the importance of this issue. Some teachers would penalize a student with a lower grade; others might say, if the student can demonstrate mastery of content without the camera or microphone, it can stay off. You need to decide *if* mastery can be shown without those pieces. Unless your school has rules/guidelines around this issue, it is up to you, the teacher, to decide.

UNIT 5: WHAT ARE CHOICE BOARDS, AND HOW TO USE THEM IN YOUR DIGITAL SPACE

C hoice boards, also known as Learning Menus, are a fantastic way to increase engagement, address differentiated learning, and make your lessons student centered. Choice boards encourage students to be independent and take responsibility and ownership of their learning, even in the earliest grades.

A choice board can be as simple as a chart in a Google doc, with a link to an activity that relates to the big idea and essential question you presented in your lesson. While all the activities are reinforcing the main idea, skill, or theme of your lesson, they address different ways of reinforcement: one choice might be further reading and answering questions. Another might be watching a video and recording a video response for submission. Another might ask the student to draw a picture/write a poem/compose a song or rap to restate the big ideas. The two major components of each choice on the board are: further explanation the student can access him/herself, and an activity that reinforces learning and can show the teacher if the student under-stands or needs more guidance. Elementary Choice Boards normally have a chart with 3-5 choices, older students may have 8-12 choices. Making these charts can be time consuming up front, but remember, the charts can be reused over a period of days, and students can choose different activities each day.

- Choice boards, also known as learning menus, give students ownership and extends your big ideas
- Choice boards address differentiated learning in your classroom
- Choice boards, a student centered activity, increase student engagement and contribute to higher learning retention

UNIT 6: MORE THAN VIRTUAL PENPALS: PARTNERING WITH ANOTHER CLASS ONLINE

There are several digital platforms, like ePals and PenPal Schools (which became free when the pandemic hit in spring 2020), that are dedicated to connecting classes and student groups by age, content area, and interests. This is a terrific way to add a worldwide perspective and diversity to your class, whatever you teach. From the distance teaching perspective, imagine how your knowledge base could expand by talking to distance educators from another country. The benefits include increased opportunity for writing in the classroom, improved writing and communication skills, opportunities for diversity and inclusivity awareness, and heightened social studies and geography skills. Sites like SkypeForClassroom and StudentsOfTheWorld offer safe options for matching your class to another.

- Depending on the age and size of your virtual class, you want to choose if Snail Mail, Email, or Video Chat is the best way to connect with another virtual classroom
- Benefits of Virtual PenPals include strengthening writing skills (if you choose traditional mail or email), which addresses language arts standards, or public speaking skills and possibly foreign language experience

- Students will gain exposure to another culture, either international or domestic, depending on the location of your PenPals

UNIT 7: HOW TO ADD A VIRTUAL FIELD TRIP TO YOUR CURRICULUM

When you are distance teaching, obviously field trips cannot happen in person, and field trips are widely known to be an essential part of the educational experience. Field trips do not have to be dropped from your school year during distance teaching. Many companies and organizations cater to making distance learning field trips an enriching activity for students in all grades.

- Several Zoos around the country, including the San Diego Zoo, the Houston Zoo, and the Cincinnati Zoo offer live feeds of animal activities, some on a weekly basis. The Atlanta Zoo has a livestream of their PandaCam, and they can also learn what the panda keepers do to keep the pandas happy and healthy.
- The Louvre Museum in Paris houses some of the most famous works of art in the world. The museum offers several tours of their priceless works, including the Egyptian Sphinx, the Winged Victory and the Mona Lisa. There is also Psyche Revived by Cupid's Kiss and The Raft of the Medusa, all of which lend themselves nicely to interdisciplinary activities.

- Explore outer space without NASA training! Students can visit both the surface of Mars and the International Space Station through virtual field trips powered by the NASA website.
- Your class can visit five National Parks at Google Arts and Culture National Parks. Fjords, volcanos, shipwrecks...students can fly with bats, dive with a National Park ranger to explore coral reefs, and see the inside of a volcano without getting burned.
- Hike three of the most famous spots of the Great Wall of China -- over 3,000 miles long-- without the long flight. Students will learn about the culture and history of the region and see breathtaking, 360 degree views from the Great Wall itself.
- Two wonderful virtual field trips that work well together are the Statue of Liberty tour and the Ellis Island Museum Tour. Learn the history of immigration as well as the building of the emblem of freedom the immigrants saw when they came to America. The Statue tour includes views from the Crown, which has been closed to the public for several decades.
- Tour the White House, with narration by former President Obama. In addition you can see the Old Executive Office Building (OEOB), and learn about Presidential and First Lady history, decor, and family life. This tour was also made possible through Google Arts and Culture.
- Take a royal tour of Buckingham Palace, the official residence of the Queen of England, Elizabeth the Second. You can visit three separate parts of the Palace, the Throne Room, the Grand Staircase, and the White Drawing Room. During the tour you will also find interesting information about the royal family, their charity work, famous people who have visited the palace, and the events and ceremonies that take place at the Palace every year.

UNIT 8: HOW TO USE SOCIAL MEDIA AS PART OF YOUR DISTANCE TEACHING PLAN

What sets social media apart from other media is that social media is *two way communication.* Information can be sent *and* received. Social media has become reliable, free, simple, and widespread. While social media is used often by the younger crowd for informal chat and posting duck-faced selfies, social media can be used responsibly and professionally. Many teachers teaching traditionally and from a distance use social media in a variety of ways. For example, making a text group for students and another for parents is a great way to publish important deadline reminders, class events, or just check in. Some teachers set up a Twitter handle specifically for this reason, others use the text feature on their smartphones. There are several free apps available like Remind that allow you to communicate with groups without making your private information, like a phone number, public. If you don't want to do those, you can set up an email group using your school email account to write notes quickly and send to everyone in one click.

If you decide to go 'old school,' as student aged kids consider it today, you can still create a private group on FaceBook and decide whether or not to allow members other than yourself (the administrator) to post and/or comment. FaceBook is free, teachers today are probably familiar with it and have an account, so there would be no learning curve.

- Remember that social media can be used in professional ways
- Social media is an easy way for students and families to connect with you, and for you to remind your learning community about deadlines and events in your class
- If you are going to use social media to help with classroom communication, pay *very* close attention to your privacy settings

UNIT 9: THE ULTIMATE GOAL: HOW TO CREATE SELF SUFFICIENT DISTANCE LEARNERS

As much as we all want to simply dive into our opening activity, SEL activity, content, and student centered activities, when a tech related issue will stop us in our tracks. Someone's microphone won't unmute, a program won't open, or a screen is 'glitchy.' Suddenly the distance teacher is also the IT department, thinking, when will these students be self sufficient on their devices? Hopefully, they are on simple Chromebooks provided by the district so you have the backup you need, but for smaller issues, we need to be teaching our students how to troubleshoot so these small issues don't stop you from teaching. The bigger message/issue is....a teacher should not become a crutch in any way. Teaching students to be independent is a goal for every teacher. So if you hear constant complaints about tech problems, be ready with some simple solutions the students can go to themselves. In fact, having these guidelines in your class outline or posted in your digital classroom is another good idea.

- To begin, always ask the student, Have you tried restarting? Nine times out of ten a re-start will take care of a computer issue. A restart triggers a checklist in the computer's brain, so if any important component has 'clicked off,' a restart will click it back on.

- Tell the student to restart the router/modem in their home (ask if an adult or older sibling can help).
- Check their connections. Perhaps a wire has slipped loose, and this is an easy solution that should not steal your teaching time.
- Check that the headphones/keyboard/mouse/anything that is plugged in is plugged into the correct place.
- Students should know in advance to go through these steps before alerting you to a problem. If, *after* they have done all of the above steps, then you can set aside time to help the student. But usually, these steps will fix the problem and most students can do them unassisted.

CONCLUSION: YOU'VE GOT THIS

Distance teaching may feel like an overwhelming task. Some days it will be. It is similar to traditional brick and mortar teaching that way. What gives distance teaching meaning, and increases your feeling of reward, is the connection and relationship this particular style of teaching brings. Additionally, when your focus is on community, engagement, and connection, teaching the content becomes 1) streamlined, 2) simpler, and 3) doubly rewarding, because you see the connections happening with your students in real time. When you can build that positive, aspirational environment in your classroom, you will have students who want to log in and show up in every definition of that phrase. Connection and engagement reduces classroom management issues and raises content retention and deeper understanding.

If you came into teaching because you want to educate children and young adults and help make the education system better, *you are in the right place at the right time.*

Some thoughts to sustain you on the harder days...

- The secret to getting ahead is getting started. --Mark Twain
- It's hard to beat a person who never gives up. --Babe Ruth

- The hard days are what make you stronger. --Aly Raisman
- Work hard, be kind, and amazing things will happen. --Conan O'Brien
- In the middle of every difficulty is opportunity. --Albert Einstein

SEL & GROWTH MINDSET RESOURCES

www.stormprogram.com/sel

MR E'S MYSTERIES

Mr. E's Mysteries is a fun and educational video series which leads students on an exploration of emotions, and provides educators with the tools they need to establish a positive class culture.

SEL Video Series with Weekly Activities

Any student can be a role model, but sometimes negative emotions can lead us to make poor choices. Students will join the detective Mr. E, in trying to identify what emotions our zany characters are experiencing when they make certain choices.

Students will also explore different strategies to cope with and express difficult feelings in a positive and healthy way.

BOX INCLUDES

- 5 interactive videos exploring the characteristics of kindness, integrity, perseverance, self-control, and responsibility
- 25 classroom activities (5 activities per characteristic) to practice each character quality.
- A full set of wristbands and certificates to be awarded to students who earn them.

S.T.O.R.M. TEAM

Parents and educators alike want their kids to be happy, healthy and successful. It's a personal mission woven into their very being. It's a mission that can only be achieved by empowering our youth to make their own positive choices, the same positive choices that will make them Role Models.

As a S.T.O.R.M.™ certified school. You will get all the necessary tools to operate a storm program at your site.

The S.T.O.R.M.™ Team School is a system designed to support the development of the whole child. On-boarding, support and certification will be provided to selected teachers. This process will include access to a library of online professional development videos to assist them in facilitating powerful S.T.O.R.M.™ lessons.

Each lesson contains challenging missions for students in the areas of fitness, nutrition, and social-emotional learning.

INCLUDED

- Staff training
- Lesson plans (42 weeks)
- Video tutorials
- Achievement medals

STORME

Teachers carry with them a tremendous amount of responsibility and demands on their time. So much so, they are constantly challenged to prioritize how they will spend that time. The most successful teachers prioritize their relationships with their students.

180 Days Of SEL Mindful Exercises

STORMe: Mindful Exercises is a system and a daily curriculum designed to create a powerful, fun, and safe space in the classroom to build a sense of belonging for students. It is to build a belief among students that they are part of a team. By taking 3 – 5 minutes every day teachers will act with intention to strengthen not only the teacher-student relationship, but all of the student-to-student relationships in their classroom. Backed with support of their teammates, students will be better equipped to tackle the many challenges they face throughout the school day.

INCLUDED

- Staff training
- Lesson plans (42 weeks)
- Video tutorials
- Achievement medals

NO WARIES

No Waries™ is a fast-paced exciting social emotional learning game for kids. Kids and adults alike can grow frustrated when they are unable to express or even identify what they are feeling.

The aim of this game is to empower kids with a stronger emotional vocabulary, and equip them with the ability to describe a vast array of feelings. This will lead them to feel more successful and less frustrated.

Based on the classic card game War, players will be challenged to use a wide variety of emotions vocabulary words.

War game that helps players understand 110 different emotions.

BENEFITS

- Start the day off with positivity
- Build belief and strong class culture
- Explore the six Character Pillar of Caring, Trustworthiness, Respect, Responsibility, Fairness, & Citizenship
- Practice Social Emotional Learning
- Develop tools to overcome the many adversities students face in the classroom
- Packet Includes
- Daily Curriculum (5 minute lessons) for 180 school days
- Posters (to serve as a visual aid for students of their daily themes)
- Teamwork Trackers (to collect data on the efforts of students to be a good teammate)

MATCH MASTER

Match Master™ is a captivating social emotional learning game for kids. Being able to precisely identify your emotions is a key component in emotional maturity and essential to practicing restorative justice. This game inspires conversations about emotions and helps players to develop their emotional vocabulary so they are better able to express themselves.

Match emotions and expand your SEL vocabulary.

In the game, players must match wacky, animated faces displaying a wide range of emotions. With each matching pair, players will also find two words describing the emotion: one common word, and a more advanced word. To earn points, players must describe when they have felt that emotion.

BENEFITS

This card game helps children.

- Develop stronger language and vocabulary skills to better describe their emotions
- Differentiate between similar emotions like sad and lonely
- Express their feelings with words
- Improves critical thinking and listening skills
- Promote social bonding with classmates, friends, and family
- Develop a relationship and share more about themselves when working one-on-one with a counselor, mentor, or a teacher.
- Have fun while learning

EMOJINATION

This imaginative dice game challenges kids to tap into their emotions to build their own picture story.

We all experience difficult emotions like anger, sadness, and fear. These are natural and normal. If we take a look at the big picture though, we can see that mad can lead us to motivated, sadness to strength, and fear to focus.

To get there, you'll need to build your own story.

Learn SEL through story telling.

BENEFITS

This lively and entertaining game helps kids...

- Process difficult emotions like anger , sadness, and fear
- Practice critical thinking
- Exercise creativity
- Develop their story telling ability
- Recognize their own strengths
- Communicate their own feelings using words
- Build their sense of empathy for others
- Learn that they have choices when reacting to difficult emotions

SEL BOOK

20 ways to implement social emotional learning in your classroom is written by an educational coach and 5 time black belt master trainer Ka'ren Minasian.

20 ways to implement SEL in your classroom

You will gain practical strategies for teaching social-emotional learning (SEL) in your classroom, and help your students maintain positive relationships, be more responsible, self aware, respectful and contributing citizens of society.

You'll find easy to follow lessons and activities that will give you the tools to positively transform your classroom while Boosting Class Morale & Academic Achievement.

SECTIONS

The book is broken down into 3 categories

SEL AS A CLASS

1. Cultivate kindness in the classroom
2. Teach students positive phrases to help them be resilient through failures
3. Create anchor charts with your students
4. Role-play to develop empathy
5. Reflect on the day to see how kids are feeling and set goals for the next day

TEAMS, PARTNERSHIPS, AND GROUPS

PERSONAL CONNECTIONS, INTROSPECTION, AND STUDY

Made in the USA
Monee, IL
16 August 2021